Will You Sit Here & Die?

APOSTLE ROBBIN HARGROVE

DEDICATION

I dedicate this book to God the Father, the Son and the Holy Ghost. May you get the glory for all that I say and do and be well pleased with my life.

TABLE OF CONTENTS

ACKNOWLEDGMENTS

A very special thank you to my spiritual mother, Apostle Kim A. Davis, for providing me with Pastoral training and guidance with a spirit of excellence, a huge smile and a warm connection. A heartfelt thank you to Chief Apostle Eugene Smith, my spiritual father, who has helped me to see that you must RUN with vision and never walk with it. Thank you for your wisdom, compassion and unconditional love. To Apostle Herb & Pastor Lois Hutchinson, thank you for covering me while I recovered from hurt and disappointment. Thank you for the creative anointing and global vision that you have imparted into me. Thank you to D.E.E.P for helping me polish all of my diamonds and pearls. Thank you to The Embassy for your support in all I do. Thank you to my family, John Earl Hargrove III, Zinia, John Earl IV, Danajha and Myriah, for loving me and supporting me in ministry despite your personal lives. Thank you to Rhonda Williams for being the best friend anyone could have. Most of all, thank you to my mother, Pastor Peaches Bedford and my grandmother, Dr. Alberta Johnson, for laying my foundation for ministry and showing me a true example of Kingdom unity, love and perseverance. I'm grateful for the long days and nights in service and the unadulterated Word of God brought forth in my youth. I love you both.

APOSTLE ROBBIN HARGROVE

INTRODUCTION

As long as you still have a body of flesh, you will always be at war with what your flesh wants to do and what the spirit of God is telling you to do. We have to get to a place of not only being obedient, but having a firm understanding that we have come too far to give up or turn around. We can no longer look back from where we have come from and entertain the desire to go back. Looking back can cost you everything, just ask Lot's wife. Genesis 19:26 says, *"But his wife looked back and became a pillar of salt."* Your walk with God has to be constant and ever moving forward. Even if you are moving at a snail's pace, KEEP MOVING!!!

APOSTLE ROBBIN HARGROVE

Chapter One:
WILL YOU SIT HERE AND DIE?

As a new pastor (shepherd) I had to quickly learn the characteristics of the congregation (sheep). And just like people, sheep come in all different shapes, sizes, and personalities. Some sheep come for a short time. Their contribution to the flock is often minimal. Some sheep come to stay and whether they are productive or not, we know that they are dependable and will be there. But some sheep are actually wolves in sheep's clothing. Their agenda is often hidden and never prospers the growth of the ministry. Their deception is often damaging as its evidence is seen in the broken hearts and lack of trust they leave in their wake.

After coming into contact with the latter, I found myself in this very place. It is a place I was all too familiar with. A wolf had used its means of stealth and cunning wit, and had managed to steal some of the sheep that I was extremely fond of. You may think that as a pastor I should be able to just get over it, dust myself off and keep it moving. You may think I should be able to just shake it off, especially since there are still so many other sheep in need of direction. Proverbs 4:23 tells me,

"Keep thy heart with all diligence; for out of it are the issues of life."

But the fact of the matter is, it hurts.

Each morning I wake up, I make a decision to fellowship and commune with God. Usually, I'm excited to hear from the Father what my daily instructions are and how He will direct me in my day. My response to His will is usually "I'm for hire!" But because my heart had been broken, on this particular Monday morning, I lay in the bed with my hurt and discomfort. As the Lord began to minister to me, my response was to just lay there in silence. I had begun to shut down. I didn't want to speak and I didn't want to be spoken to. I wasn't happy and I felt that I was entitled to not push myself that day and furthermore, the Lord should understand. It was then that I heard the Holy Spirit say to me, "Will you sit here and die?"

I knew exactly where He was coming from, but instead of celebrating in and for the presence of the God, I gave no answer as I pulled the covers over my head and rolled over. Now remember that the Holy Spirit is a gentleman and will not force himself upon you. It was only after I could no longer feel His presence that I cried out to God, asking this question; "How can I have a pastor's heart for the people and at the same time effectively guard it? How do I love the people, engage in spiritual warfare for the people, pray for the people and their families and still guard my heart so that I'm not reacting to what they do?" But I heard nothing.

Every second and third Tuesday of the month I minister the word of God in a service known as "Date Night with Jesus". Women from all over South Jersey, Delaware and Philadelphia travel to fellowship with their sisters and worship our Savior. Well, I didn't feel like it. I didn't feel like going on a date and I didn't feel like preaching. What I wanted to do was cancel the service. Can I be real with you? What I wanted to do was to get back in the bed with the covers pulled over my head and call out sick. But I couldn't do that. There are no personal days, or sick time or vacation time that you can use when there is an assignment on your life. I had an assignment and I still had to show up. As I was driving, I had to ask God for forgiveness and mercy since I didn't feel like going. I was in great need of his reassurance that what I was doing was really making a difference.

I began to look over my options. I could stay home and do nothing, but that would more than likely produce nothing. I could give up the ministry and concentrate my efforts in corporate America. I was always pretty good there, but I was never truly fulfilled. It seemed as if every option I had was a bad option with a negative return. I needed to hear from God. I needed a miracle. The miracle I needed wasn't about paying bills or a way out of no way. This was about being straight up heartbroken and discouraged. I had looked to my counselors and looked to my spiritual coverings, but they weren't available. They had issues, tissues and puffs of their own I guess.

Mind you, all this is taking place during my 30-minute drive to church. So again, I looked to God and asked the same question I had asked earlier, but this time He responded. His response was to repeat the same question he had asked earlier that day, "Will you sit here and die?" It was then that I realized that even if you have what you deem to be bad options, you still have options. I didn't like my options. They all seemed to have consequences. They were all a gamble. But I had options.

Chapter Two:
YOU'VE GOT LEPROSY

In 2 Kings 7:3, the bible talks about four leprous men who sat at the gate of the city to Samaria. Due to their "unclean and contagious" physical condition they could not interact with clean citizens. Their future seemed bleak and they began to weigh their options.

Option 1. They could enter into the city, but because there was a great famine in the land they determined that they could die of starvation.

Option 2. Their second option was to

go to their enemy, the Syrian army, and surrender. They knew this was a gamble because the Syrians would either let them live as prisoners or they would kill them. They considered that even if they lived out the remains of their lives as prisoners, at least they would be fed.

There were two choices and both choices came with an *"IF"* clause. *If* we do this, we could starve to death and *If* we do that, our enemy might kill us. What do you do when you are stuck between a rock and a hard place? Consider this, some of the things we go through do not hover between life and death. Usually the things we trip over and fall out about won't cost us our lives. Yet our head is all messed up and crazy as if our very lives are in the balance. I tell my congregation all the time, "let it go, so you can grow." If your children are alive, if you have good health, if there is a roof over your head, if someone loves you, then you should be celebrating. And even if you think you can't find something to give God glory for, if you woke up in the land of the living, then you are still a living, breathing miracle and that alone deserves a "thank you God." When you are face to face with whatever is plaguing your thought process, I want you to remember Philippians 4:8-9 as it reads,

"Finally brethren, whatsoever things are true, whatsoever things are honest, whatsoever things are just, whatsoever things are pure, whatsoever things are of good report: if there be any virtue, and if there be any praise, think on these things. Those things, which ye have both learned, and received, and

heard, and seen in me, do: and the God of peace shall be with you."

Despite your situation, God is still in control and deserving of your heartfelt joyful noise.

So, at the gate, we have four men. The number four represents seasons. On the fourth day, God created the sun, moon, and stars. They are the instruments of time. Our study of them has given us days and nights, which lead into months and years and seasons. In Hebrew, the word *season* can be translated as *"appointed time"*. This refers to God's appointed times which are His Holy Feast times (the feast of unleavened bread, the feast of weeks, and the feast of tabernacles). Have you ever noticed that when you are in a particular season in your life that you seem to attract and are attracted to people who share the characteristics of your season? In the summer, people with vacation on their minds flock in droves to the beach for surf and fun. During a dry season, everyone is looking for water. If you are in a season of joy, then you want to be around people who are joyful. And even if you are in a season of struggle you seem to find comfort in being around those who have the same struggle. They can't judge you because for the most part, they are reacting to the struggle in the same manner you are. When you are in a "mood", you want to be with people that are like minded. If you manage to make it to church and you still don't feel like worshipping, you look for the people who are wearing their struggle and are not worshipping so at least you can fit in. In a sense, they co-sign your mess and you co-sign theirs.

Leprosy is a chronic, long term disease. It is a highly contagious flesh-eating bacterium. The bacterium that causes leprosy is contracted through an airborne droplet coming from a sneeze or cough. It mainly affects the skin, but can also affect the eyes, nose, and peripheral nervous system (all the nerves outside the brain and spinal cord). Have you ever wondered how you could wake up feeling joyous and then sit next to someone or be in a room with someone that's not having a good day, and before you know it, you no longer have the joy you started the day with? Their leprous condition has affected the very atmosphere of the room! And because leprosy is contagious, you have contracted what they have.

There is a significance to where the four leprous men were sitting. They were sitting at the gate. Keep in mind that **YOU** are the church, **I** am the church, and **WE** are the church. The Lord is not coming back looking for a building. Our gates grant access. Access to your church should only be granted to men and women according to their God given assignment in your life. Sometimes people who are leprous in their spirit will sit at your gate. Their mindset is contemplating whether they will die now or die later, but nonetheless their mind is fixed on death. I know you are wondering why am I talking about leprosy. You may not feel like you have leprosy and you are not a negative person, but if you have ever been heartbroken and hurt like I was, then let's take a look at this in the spiritual realm.

Sometimes you go through rough situations and as a result you find yourself speaking negatively, bitterly and nasty; guess what, you have leprosy and your speech is a sign that it is eating away at you. You are leprous when you make your flesh the deciding factor between giving God glory or not. You are leprous when your flesh is the deciding factor between you obeying God's will or not. You are leprous when you make your flesh the deciding factor between you believing what thus saith the Lord thy God or not. The keyword here again is "if". "If" you will or "if" you won't. "If" you do or "if'" you don't. Spiritually, obedience is a life or death situation. If Jonah never prayed while inside the big fish, how much longer do you think he would have been in there? When your flesh puts an "if" in your mind in place of faith, then you have leprosy, and it's contagious.

We find ourselves wanting to call anyone that will listen to our sad stories. Our issue makes us bitter because we are sick and tired of being sick and tired. And subconsciously we do not want others to get ahead, especially if it means leaving us behind. And everyone who gets too close can be exposed to our nasty talking, stinkin' thinkin' selves. All because the leprosy you contracted was positioned at the gate.

Chapter Three:
WHAT ARE THE OPTIONS?

The four leprous men are talking to each other and one of them decides to weigh their options. It only takes one. Will you be the one to recognize your options? Can you look beyond your issues, tissues, and puffs and recognize that you have the potential to save yourself and others? Don't get caught up as you look into the eyes of your situation, but rather begin to change your perspective. Change your thinking in order to figure out what can be done about your circumstance. Once the one leper changed the conversation, the others began to consider their options in a new light. Sometimes all we need to do, is start a new conversation.

During the conversation, you will find that some people will actually choose to remain in a spirit of discontent. Some people will choose to remain in Lodebar (a place of no hope, desolation, and forgotten people). Some people have become content with the pity party because they feel that the pain, violation, and embarrassment they have suffered entitles them to extra attention and excuses them from moving on. They think that the existence of these issues validates their decision to stay in their leprous state. But **YOU** must make the decision to evict yourself from Lodebar and absolutely refuse to die! Begin to look over all the promises in the bible and count your blessings. Look at all that God has brought you through and make a decision to keep living and live on purpose with a purpose. Remember what God did for Israel; remember the prophetic words spoken over and into your life. Hold God to His word and remember this too shall pass. Then stand up and refuse to die for your story is not yet over.

They examined their options. Their first option was to go into Samaria. But because the famine was so great they found that people had actually begun to eat each other's infants for food. I call it the "I'm gonna eat your baby famine." Sometimes things can get so rough that people will eat their own seed in order to survive. They can get so desperate to feed their flesh that they can eat the very seed that's planted on the inside of themselves. I know no one will literally eat their baby in this present time, but people will move their children out of position because of their situation. And because of their leprous state, they are willing to gamble on their children's lives and move them away from the calling of God that is on their lives. Often, they move to where there is no God so that not only do they starve, but they cause their children to starve also. People can get so nasty that they begin to kill off their children's spirit with a language of leprosy that is spoken into the lives of the ones closest to them. I'll be honest, I've had times where I've allowed my flesh to speak on my behalf and found that it was an assassination to my own house.

If you read 2 Kings, chapter 6, you will find that the people were so desperate for food that they were selling dove's dung and donkey heads for consumption. One woman convinced her neighbor to boil her son for food and then hid her son, whom she promised for food the next day. They were in a perilous situation due to their disobedience to God. An unwilling spirit can cause a famine and bring a dry season.

Their second option was to visit the enemy's camp and gamble with their very lives. The Syrians had overcome them in war for so long that the Syrian's possessions were actually belongings of Samaria which they had obtained as spoils of war. Aren't you tired of the enemy benefiting at your expense? There are some things that you have allowed the enemy to do to you. You hear a negative report about someone and it changes your mind about them. Isn't it funny how we never seek the words of the "offender" and possibly gain a word of truth, but rather allow a lie to steer us away from someone who has a God given assignment in our life or even steer us away from the house of God that He Himself planted us in? Will you continue to allow the enemy to walk in, divide and conquer you because you won't seek the truth?

As we read, we find that they decide to go into the camp of their enemy (the Syrians). Isn't it something to have to put your life in the hands of your enemy? Ironically, sometimes your enemy is the best way out because it's the people who you trust most, who have access to you, that have it in for you. The four men began their journey at twilight. Why is twilight significant? Twilight is either the dawning of a new day or the end of one. It is the time where the sun is either rising or setting. Scientist believe that when we are looking at the sunset, the sun is actually already below the horizon. But because of the way light bends in the atmosphere, it allows us to see the sun around the curvature of the earth. This is called an optical illusion. There are some things that happen quickly at twilight. When we celebrate the Hebrew feast, we begin at twilight or sundown. Time really begins at twilight!

My point is, when the sun is appearing to be going down, it's time for you to move. As soon as you come to the end of a day you must make a decision what your next day will look like. You can't wait until the dawning of a new day or when you wake up because your new day is really birthed out at sunset. I figured we've had it backwards all this time. Don't wait until the morning because the enemy is already in position and strategizing against you while you are sleeping. If you always feel like your timing is off, this is the reason.

Chapter Four:
MAKE THE DECISION

The hardest part of this process is making the decision to move. This is especially true when you are trying to move from a nasty attitude to a positive one. The leprous men decided to take themselves to the enemy's camp and they began to move. We spend more time and more energy in debate trying to decide if we will simply move. We often mask our indecisiveness with "meditation" and we're waiting to hear from God. But the truth is we just don't want to move. The bible says we should meditate on the scriptures day and night and if we were active in this meditation we would find that we don't have time for meditating on our own thoughts that are leading us nowhere. Make a decision on what you are going to do from here right now!

So, the men left towards the camp and when they arrived at their destination, to their surprise there was no one there. The enemy's camp was empty. Here's the thing, while you are making a decision about dying, God is has already made a decision about you living. He's just waiting on you.

2 Kings 7:6-7 speaks of how God had caused the army of the Syrians to hear noises that sounded like horses and chariots. The Syrian army said to themselves that the King of Israel had hired another King and his army to fight

against them and they fled leaving all the spoils of the camp intact. God has been causing your enemy to hear things that no one else hears. And he is removing your enemy and returning all that was lost. Remember the Lord is always on your side and there is more of us than there are of them. There is a sound that will come from Heaven and turn your situation around. When the Syrians heard these sounds, they fled at twilight. Yes, the very same twilight when the lepers moved. All you have to do is make a decision. When you move in, your enemy will have to move out. Your giant will fall, your red sea will part, and your enemy will depart from your presence, but only when you move.

Chapter Five:
TAKE IT BACK & SHARE

The lepers arrived at the Syrian camp and found that there was no one there. They began to eat of the food until their stomachs were filled. Then they began to lay hold of the spoils of war that had been deserted and they hid them throughout the camp. Wait a minute!!! If you were planning on dying, then why are you hiding jewels? Why build a savings account if you are going to die and never use the money saved? Their action is an indication that their mindset had changed. When you decide to move, you are not just changing your position, you are also changing within your mind. God changed their entire perspective at twilight and He is still doing the same for others and will do the same for you today. He won't just shift your mind to wanting to live, but He will shift it so that you are thinking about your future. It's when you think about how significant your unknown future is, that you begin to want back all you've lost in the past. I want it all back, everything that was taken, everything that was stolen, everything that I lost, everything that I forfeited, no matter what it was and no matter what happened or why it is that I no longer have it, **I WANT IT BACK!!!**

They went from tent to tent, finding things and storing them for later. As you read this chapter, I want you to go through the recesses of your mind and contemplate the things you may have lost. Then as you move in your position and in your mind, make a decision to take back everything that is missing. Have you lost your joy? **TAKE IT BACK!** Have you lost your peace? **TAKE IT BACK!** Have you lost a relationship with a loved one? **TAKE IT BACK!** Make up your mind to take back the things that belong to you. If you are still alive in this season, then begin to realize that you are exiting a season of famine and death and you are entering a new season of plenty and life.

In the 9th verse, the four men realized that there was something not quite right about all this and that there was no one around to share their experience with. They were the only ones enjoying the spoils. Isn't that just like us to experience a great breakthrough and never tell a soul? Or we talk about it only with those who already knew the story. Why don't we have the mindset to share with everyone what God has done for us? The world needs to know the awesome power and deep love of our God. As saints, we need to realize that no matter what the calamity, God has already worked a miracle on our behalf. The four lepers knew that if they waited until the morning light, it would be too late. There are some things in your life that you don't have a tomorrow for. Some things just won't wait. You must get them in order NOW! It is possible that tomorrow will never come. Tomorrow just might be too late. We wonder why we find ourselves back in dire situations time after time. We never realize that God is giving us another opportunity to get it right and give Him the glory He deserves for again pulling us out of the pit in our life. We must tell our stories and shine the light on the one who is responsible for bringing us out. Our testimonies can inspire, encourage, confirm, and bring hope to someone who thinks it's hopeless.

Chapter Six:
SUSPICIOUS LEADERSHIP

In verse 10, they went to the gatekeepers of the city and told them about the empty Syrian camp. But the King was suspicious. If you are a leader within the gates, you have to remember to check your mindset. We can't afford to always be suspicious of everyone. We cannot afford to prejudge people.

Yes, you have been betrayed. Yes, you have been lied on. Yes, you have lent your last only to never see that individual again. Yet we cannot afford to shut the gates. When someone we don't know is bringing us good news, we should be able to try the spirit by the spirit and determine if the spirit is of God. 1 Corinthians 1:27 reads,

"God uses the foolish things of the world to confound the wise; and God has chosen the weak things of the world to confound the things which are mighty. And base things of the world, and things which are despised, has God chosen, yes, and things which are not, to bring to naught things that are:"

Leadership must be able to get over their past and let the new people in. There will be people who come to you lacking the worldly appearance of success, yet these are the very people that God will use in this season to deliver a message while bearing great gifts.

As this is of great importance I repeat, we cannot afford to live under the influence of a hardened heart to the point that our hearts (which was once a place that had room for everyone) now has a No-Vacancy sign on the front door. Don't get stuck there. Don't get stuck with a negative mindset. Make it your business to have a personal heart to heart with the Lord and allow Him to show you how to deal with those whom He has sent and those who were sent by someone else.

Chapter Seven:
RUNNERS

Here we find the king receiving wise counsel from one of his servants. The servant says to the King that there are only a few Israelites who remain in the city and in the entire city there were only five horses left. The servant proposed to the king that he should send some men along with the five horses to investigate the Syrian camp to better judge the lepers story. And if something happened to the men and horses, be it good or bad, it's most likely the same would fall upon those that remain in Israel.

You have to begin to fully understand that your decision (mindset) is your determining factor as to whether you will blend in with the crowd or if you will make the shift to set you apart and eventually lead the masses. God promised that Israel would be set apart. Israel is not to have the same speech, the same appearance, the same custom or culture. We have a decision to make; either we are going to be consumed like the rest of the people or we are going to rise above this thing. Today more than ever, there are pastors that are walking out of the house of God. They are closing their doors and fleeing from their assignment. I can admit to being a runner in the past. Keeping my bag packed at all times, knowing how to get away on little to no money at all. But God said to me, "Will you run and be consumed and look just like everyone else or will you finally stand here flat footed and toe to toe and know that what, "I the Lord thy God, has promised shall come to pass?"

We must remember that God does not operate in time. What he has planned for your life actually has already been done. We have yet to see the full manifestation of his promises because we have the bad habit of throwing in the towel too soon. And because He has already worked it out in my favor, I can rejoice knowing that those things that appear to have the potential to destroy me are only optical illusions because **"All things work together for GOOD to them that love God, to them who are the called according to his purpose."** (Romans 8:28)

Chapter Eight:
JUST SHOW UP

In the eighth chapter, we find a Shunamite woman who paid attention to the prophet. She asked her husband to build a room because she believed him to be a man of God. After such, the prophet Elisha spoke into the woman's life. She went through a process and eventually gave birth to a son only to watch her seed die. Instead of merely receiving the cards life dealt her, she shifted her mindset to finding the man of God that he might restore what had been lost. This is an example of faith in action. Elisha did in fact bring her son back to life and her faith was increased. When you have a prophet in the house, he or she can foretell what is to come so that you don't have to experience everything that everyone else does. As I am writing this book, I want the reader to know that what happens in everyday life to you, I experience also. You are not alone. We all go through it. 1 Corinthians 10:13 reads,

*"There hath no temptation taken you but such as is **common** to man: but God is faithful, who will not suffer you to be tempted above that ye are able; but will with the temptation also make a way to escape, that ye may be able to bear it."*

We all suffer through famine and endure through different trials in our lives. There is stuff with the kids, stuff with our spouses, stuff at work, stuff with money, stuff with the person who cut you off in traffic, just stuff stuff stuff! No one is immune to it. It's just how you deal with it that makes the difference. So, the prophet told her to pack her stuff and her household and get her family out of the land. In other words he told her to MOVE! And where did she go you ask? She moved into the Philistines camp (the enemy's camp). Can you see a pattern here? When the four lepers moved, they moved into the camp of their Syrian enemies and when the Shunamite woman moved, she moved into the camp of her enemy, the Philistines. But even as God moved when the lepers moved, God also moved when the Shunamite woman moved. She left everything she had. She left her house, her land, and her people. It cost her something to be able to survive the famine. It cost her to be obedient. It looked like what she left behind was lost, but what she didn't realize was that God had already made the way.

At some point her story is being told to the king and at the same time she *shows up* and requests an audience of the king. The King then grants her a return of all she had lost and more. God had already made provision for her and He's doing the same for you today. It's all because she *showed up.* Sometimes the hardest part is showing up.

I recently attended an award ceremony and because of a storm in my life I almost didn't go. I didn't want to show up. Emotionally I was still in my bed with the covers pulled over my head. It was hard putting on my mask and smiling like everything was okay. It was a fight just to show up. That night I was the recipient of not one, not two, but three awards! The night ended with my true smile shining through as my mask was no longer needed, all because I *showed up.* I had to make a decision not to be stuck there. The blessings of our lives are waiting on us. We must *show up!*

Chapter Nine:
DIVINE APPOINTMENTS

As the servant is telling the king about the great deeds of Elisha, the Shunamite woman shows up. After being questioned by the king, the Shunamite woman confirms all that Elisha had done for her. The king then appoints a certain officer to her. When you finally get past your leprosy, when you finally get past your suspicion, when you finally get past your running, you will find yourself in a place with the king and he will appoint an officer to you and will grant to you the diplomatic rights and privileges of the kingdom. So, you better know who it is that is appointed to you and who you are connected to. It's important to know who you are assigned to and who is assigned to you in this season so you can get it all back.

The King said to restore all that was hers from the day that she had left. I decree and declare that if you just show up in this season, and don't go by what you see or by what you have heard, that God will speak over your life and order your officer to give it all back. Not just a portion, not a fraction, not a sample, but ALL! What appeared to be missing will actually earn you interest. But you must show up with the mindset that *"God is able to do exceeding abundantly above all that we ask or think, according to the power that worketh in us"* (Ephesians 3:20).

This is the season for divine partnerships and divine alliances. Don't think those ties or connections won't be tested, but understand that the fight bears witness to the divine nature of the relationship. If this thing wasn't ordained by the Father, then why is the enemy fighting it so hard?

I pray that you got something out of this book and I encourage you to stay the course and live on purpose with purpose. May God continue to bless and keep you.

For bookings & more information:
PastorRHargrove@gmail.com
www.PastorRobbin.com

Are you *pregnant* with purpose, dreams, or ministry? Birth strong with Apostle Robbin as your Spiritual Midwife! For more information, visit www.WODministries.org/register or email WomenofDeliverance@gmail.com.

Do you have a heart for infants? Help Apostle Robbin care for babies by donating new & gently used clothing to infants in crisis! Visit www.AHEARTministries.org for more information.

For help with writing and publishing books: DivineExcellenceSkills@gmail.com

ABOUT THE AUTHOR

Apostle Robbin Hargrove is an anointed Woman of God committed to evoking change to the body of Christ by building up and strengthening Ambassadors for the Kingdom of God. She is a multifaceted executive, life coach and a Spiritual Midwife Trainer. She is known for her dynamic delivery of God's Word, her keen ear for God's voice, and her authoritative blind faith in carrying out God's Word.

By the prompting of the Holy Spirit and with her love and concern for minority infants, in 2008 she founded A.H.E.A.R.T Ministries, a non-profit organization dedicated to assisting families with infants in crisis. Wherever the Lord sent her she came in contact with women who were broken spiritually and naturally. The Lord confirmed what she was feeling and The Women of Deliverance (WOD)was birthed in 2009, and the first Date Night with Jesus service was held in June 2010. She began teaching a 9-month class on Spiritual Midwives.

Apostle Kim A. Davis (Ebenezer Full Gospel Baptist Church, Downingtown, Pennsylvania) became a mentor and spiritual mother to Apostle Robbin and helped push her into her inheritance, along with her spiritual father, Chief Apostle Eugene Smith (Better Covenant International, Detroit Michigan). She became the Senior Pastor of the church her grandmother, Dr. Alberta Johnson, founded in 1977. She was blessed to have both her spiritual parents affirm her call and establish her to the office of Apostleship on August 8th, 2017.

As a victorious victim of Super Storm Hurricane Sandy, Apostle Robbin resides in New Jersey with her husband, John Hargrove III and is a loving parent to four children; Zinia, John, Danajha, and Myriah. She always gives honor to her mother, Pastor Peaches Bedford. She is proud to be known as a true woman of strong faith and prayer, striving to build God's Kingdom and reach nations!